Inspirational Journal
Self Help Book With 100 Inspiration Quotes From Famous People
(Notebook)

(Inspirational Journal To Write In)

D1367904

Other books by the author:
https://www.amazon.com/author/shalusharma
Self Discovery Journal: 121 Thought Provoking Questions
Journal for Girls: 101 Thought Provoking Questions
Journal for Boys: 101 Thought Provoking Questions
Journal for Women: 105 Questions for Women with Motivational Quotes
Spiritual Journal: 101 Spiritual Questions to Ask Yourself
Gratitude Journal: Keep a Gratitude Journal and Turn Pain to Joy
The Pregnancy Journal: Pregnancy Journal With Questions

Inspirational Quotes are important because they motivate us into achieving great things in our lives. Anytime that something in life gets tough or challenging, a motivational quote can go a long way in bringing us out of our depression and inspiring us to achieve great things. For example, if someone makes fun of you and brings your self-confidence down, the only thing that's truly bringing your confidence down is your acceptance of what the other person says. Just refer back to the following inspirational quote by Eleanor Roosevelt, "No one can make you feel inferior without your consent."

It isn't enough for an inspirational quote to just have a positive message. The phrases of politicians and other famous people that have been quoted for generations are remembered for a reason. The way the words are arranged and used in the quote are what really make it memorable. There must be a good mixture of psychological motivation, wordsmithing, and self-selection. This is the formula for a good inspirational quote because it has meaning and will resonate in people's minds for years to come. If you were to just use simple phrases in your motivational quotes, people would likely forget them because the words that you arranged and used are so common and forgetful. Going back to the self-confidence example, a simplified version of that quote would be something like, "You'll only feel inferior if you let people make you feel inferior." Sure, it has the same positive message, but it is not catchy and there are too many similar words used. Roosevelt's quote had a psychological impact on people's minds so they'd never forget it.

Dr. Jonathan Fader is a motivational expert and psychologist who created the Union Square Practice that is based in New York City. He believes the number of people attracted to inspirational quotes is narrowed down through a self-selection process. On top of that, if someone of higher authority tells somebody they can achieve something, the person is likely to believe it. These authority figures could be mentors, teachers, or coaches. Students look up to them as wise people and they'll likely believe whatever they say. It helps even more when these authority figures have inspirational quotes to say that are catchy and memorable too.

What you have to understand is that words have power to them. You don't necessarily need to know big words. You just have to choose words and arrange them in a certain way that sounds powerful to the listener. If you can simply express wisdom in your words and allow them to be motivating, then it will go a long way to those who hear those words. If you've ever studied Latin, then you'll understand this concept. Roughly 2,000 years ago, there were many Latin sayings floating around during those times that are still talked about today. The Latin phrase "ubi Concordia ibi Victoria" is one example of this. The English translation is "Where there is unity, there is victory." The word use of "unity" and "victory" are what make this saying so special. Not only is it a positive saying, but it is a catchy one too.

The easiest way to create an inspirational quote is to make it rhyme. In the year 2000 at Lafayette College, a group of cognitive scientists conducted a study and found that people were more likely to believe a statement that rhymed was true instead of a statement that didn't rhyme, even though they had the same overall message. In fact, attorneys use this technique all the time when trying to convince juries and/or the public of what they want them to believe. Remember the O.J. Simpson trial? One of the famous quotes to come out of that trial was by Simpson's attorney who said, "If the glove doesn't fit, you must acquit." This quote likely stuck in the minds of the jurors which could have led to their reason for acquitting Simpson in the first place.

Finally, people are attracted to inspirational quotes when they are spoken by their leaders or role models. Since human beings naturally aspire to be something better, they take the words of their leader to heart so they can improve themselves. In the minds of the people, anyone with a lot of power is likely wise because they have achieved a lot in their lives. This means anything they say must be true or have validation behind it. These aren't just leaders in politics, but also leaders in entertainment and business as well. As long as their messages are well contracted with strong appeal and imagery, then it can actually change public opinion or what people think about a particular topic in general. Celebrities and leaders both have this power and they can get away with saying virtually anything.

In this book, you will find inspirational and motivational quotes which you can read and soak in. you can write your thoughts, your ideas and anything you like in the spaces provided.

1.   You must not only aim right, but draw the bow with all your might... Henry David Thoreau

_____

_____

_____

_____

_____

_____

_____

_____

_____

_____

_____

_____

_____

_____

_____

_____

_____

_____

_____

_____

2.   Even if you're on the right track, you'll get run over if you just sit there... Will Rogers

_____

_____

_____

_____

_____

_____

_____

_____

_____

_____

_____

_____

_____

_____

_____

_____

_____

_____

_____

3.   The mind is everything. What you think you become...
Buddha

_____

_____

_____

_____

_____

_____

_____

_____

_____

_____

_____

_____

_____

_____

_____

_____

_____

_____

_____

4.   Believe you can and you're halfway there... Theodore Roosevelt

5.   You can never cross the ocean until you have the courage to lose sight of the shore... Christopher Columbus

_____

_____

_____

_____

_____

_____

_____

_____

_____

_____

_____

_____

_____

_____

_____

_____

_____

_____

_____

_____

_____

6.   I didn't fail the test. I just found 100 ways to do it wrong... Benjamin Franklin

7.   If you hear a voice within you say "you cannot paint," then by all means paint and that voice will be silenced... Vincent Van Gogh

_____

_____

_____

_____

_____

_____

_____

_____

_____

_____

_____

_____

_____

_____

_____

_____

_____

_____

_____

_____

_____

8.   However difficult life may seem, there is always
something you can do and succeed at... Stephen Hawking

_____

_____

_____

_____

_____

_____

_____

_____

_____

_____

_____

_____

_____

_____

_____

_____

_____

_____

_____

9.   I do not think that there is any other quality so essential to success of any kind as the quality of perseverance. It overcomes almost everything, even nature... John D. Rockefeller

_____

_____

_____

_____

_____

_____

_____

_____

_____

_____

_____

_____

_____

_____

_____

_____

_____

_____

10.   The two most important days in your life are the day you are born and the day you find out why... Mark Twain

_____

_____

_____

_____

_____

_____

_____

_____

_____

_____

_____

_____

_____

_____

_____

_____

_____

_____

11.   Whatever women do they must do twice as well as men to be thought half as good. Luckily, this is not difficult...
Charlotte Whitton

_____

_____

_____

_____

_____

_____

_____

_____

_____

_____

_____

_____

_____

_____

_____

_____

_____

12.   The ladder of success is best climbed by stepping on the rungs of opportunity... Ayn Rand

_____

_____

_____

_____

_____

_____

_____

_____

_____

_____

_____

_____

_____

_____

_____

_____

_____

_____

_____

13.   Great minds discuss ideas; average minds discuss events; small minds discuss people... Eleanor Roosevelt

_____

_____

_____

_____

_____

_____

_____

_____

_____

_____

_____

_____

_____

_____

_____

_____

_____

_____

_____

_____

14. The successful warrior is the average man, with laser-like focus... Bruce Lee

_____

_____

_____

_____

_____

_____

_____

_____

_____

_____

_____

_____

_____

_____

_____

_____

_____

_____

_____

_____

15.   Live as if you were to die tomorrow. Learn as if you were to live forever... Mahatma Gandhi

_____

_____

_____

_____

_____

_____

_____

_____

_____

_____

_____

_____

_____

_____

_____

_____

_____

_____

_____

_____

_____

16. The best revenge is massive success... Frank Sinatra

_____

_____

_____

_____

_____

_____

_____

_____

_____

_____

_____

_____

_____

_____

_____

_____

_____

_____

_____

_____

17.   Success is walking from failure to failure with no loss of enthusiasm... Winston Churchill

18.   It does not matter how slowly you go, so long as you do not stop... Confucius

_____

_____

_____

_____

_____

_____

_____

_____

_____

_____

_____

_____

_____

_____

_____

_____

_____

_____

_____

19.   What seems to us as bitter trials are often blessings in disguise... Oscar Wilde

_____

_____

_____

_____

_____

_____

_____

_____

_____

_____

_____

_____

_____

_____

_____

_____

_____

_____

_____

_____

_____

20.   There is only one way to avoid criticism; does nothing, say nothing, and be nothing... Aristotle

_____

_____

_____

_____

_____

_____

_____

_____

_____

_____

_____

_____

_____

_____

_____

_____

_____

_____

_____

_____

21.   Everything you can imagine is real... Pablo Picasso

_____

_____

_____

_____

_____

_____

_____

_____

_____

_____

_____

_____

_____

_____

_____

_____

_____

_____

22.   We must believe that we are gifted for something, and that this thing, at whatever cost, must be attained... Marie Curie

_____

_____

_____

_____

_____

_____

_____

_____

_____

_____

_____

_____

_____

_____

_____

_____

_____

_____

23.   Learn from yesterday, live for today, hope for tomorrow. The important thing is not to stop questioning...
Albert Einstein

24.   It is never too late to be what you might have been...
George Eliot

_____

_____

_____

_____

_____

_____

_____

_____

_____

_____

_____

_____

_____

_____

_____

_____

_____

_____

_____

25.   Education costs money. But then so does ignorance...
Sir Claus Moser

26.   One of the greatest diseases is to be nobody to anybody... Mother Teresa

_____

_____

_____

_____

_____

_____

_____

_____

_____

_____

_____

_____

_____

_____

_____

_____

_____

_____

_____

27.   When I let go of what I am, I become what I might be...
Lao Tzu

_____

_____

_____

_____

_____

_____

_____

_____

_____

_____

_____

_____

_____

_____

_____

_____

_____

_____

28.   Happiness is not something readymade. It comes from your own actions... Dalai Lama

_____

_____

_____

_____

_____

_____

_____

_____

_____

_____

_____

_____

_____

_____

_____

_____

_____

_____

_____

29.   The best time to plant a tree was 20 years ago. The second best time is now... Chinese Proverb

_____
_____
_____
_____
_____
_____
_____
_____
_____
_____
_____
_____
_____
_____
_____
_____
_____
_____
_____
_____
_____
_____

30.   It is not the strongest of the species that survive, nor the most intelligent, but the one most responsive to change... Charles Darwin

_____

_____

_____

_____

_____

_____

_____

_____

_____

_____

_____

_____

_____

_____

_____

_____

_____

_____

31.   It often requires more courage to dare to do right than to fear to do wrong... Abraham Lincoln

_____

_____

_____

_____

_____

_____

_____

_____

_____

_____

_____

_____

_____

_____

_____

_____

_____

_____

_____

_____

_____

32.   An unexamined life is not worth living... Socrates

33.   Few things can help an individual more than to place responsibility on him, and to let him know that you trust him...
Booker T. Washington

_____

_____

_____

_____

_____

_____

_____

_____

_____

_____

_____

_____

_____

_____

_____

_____

_____

_____

_____

34.   Believe you can and you're halfway there... Theodore Roosevelt

_____

_____

_____

_____

_____

_____

_____

_____

_____

_____

_____

_____

_____

_____

_____

_____

_____

_____

_____

_____

_____

35.   Fall seven times and stand up eight... Japanese Proverb

36.   Its not the years in your life that count. It's the life in your years... Abraham Lincoln

_____

_____

_____

_____

_____

_____

_____

_____

_____

_____

_____

_____

_____

_____

_____

_____

_____

_____

_____

_____

37.   I would rather die of passion than of boredom...
Vincent van Gogh

_____

_____

_____

_____

_____

_____

_____

_____

_____

_____

_____

_____

_____

_____

_____

_____

_____

_____

_____

38.   If you can dream it, you can do it... Walt Disney

39.   If your actions inspire others to dream more, learn more, do more and become more, you are a leader... John Quincy Adam

_____

_____

_____

_____

_____

_____

_____

_____

_____

_____

_____

_____

_____

_____

_____

_____

_____

_____

_____

_____

40.   If you are willing to do more than you are paid to do, eventually you will be paid to do more than you do...
Unknown

41.   If you're going to be thinking anything, you might as well think big... Donald Trump

_____
_____
_____
_____
_____
_____
_____
_____
_____
_____
_____
_____
_____
_____
_____
_____
_____
_____
_____
_____
_____
_____
_____
_____
_____

42.   Learn from yesterday, live for today, hope for tomorrow. The important thing is not to stop questioning... Albert Einstein

_____

_____

_____

_____

_____

_____

_____

_____

_____

_____

_____

_____

_____

_____

_____

_____

_____

_____

_____

_____

_____

43.   Never give up on a dream just because of the time it will take to accomplish it. The time will pass anyway... Earl Nightingale

_____

_____

_____

_____

_____

_____

_____

_____

_____

_____

_____

_____

_____

_____

_____

_____

_____

_____

_____

44.   Success usually comes to those who are too busy to be looking for it... Henry David Thoreau

_____

_____

_____

_____

_____

_____

_____

_____

_____

_____

_____

_____

_____

_____

_____

_____

_____

_____

_____

45.	Believe and act as if it were impossible to fail... Charles Kettering

_____

_____

_____

_____

_____

_____

_____

_____

_____

_____

_____

_____

_____

_____

_____

_____

_____

_____

_____

_____

46.   There is only one success, to be able to spend your life in your own way... Christopher Morley

_____

_____

_____

_____

_____

_____

_____

_____

_____

_____

_____

_____

_____

_____

_____

_____

_____

_____

47.   Failure is another steppingstone to greatness... Oprah Winfrey

_____

_____

_____

_____

_____

_____

_____

_____

_____

_____

_____

_____

_____

_____

_____

_____

_____

_____

_____

_____

_____

_____

_____

48. I believe every human has a finite number of heartbeats. I don't intend to waste any of mine... Neil Armstrong

_____

_____

_____

_____

_____

_____

_____

_____

_____

_____

_____

_____

_____

_____

_____

_____

_____

_____

49.　　Genius is 1% inspiration, 99% perspiration... Thomas Edison

_____

_____

_____

_____

_____

_____

_____

_____

_____

_____

_____

_____

_____

_____

_____

_____

_____

_____

_____

_____

_____

50.   Nothing great was ever achieved without enthusiasm...
Ralph Waldo Emerson

51.   If you don't build your dream, someone else will hire you to help them build theirs... Dhirubhai Ambani

52.   Success is not final, failure is not fatal: it is the courage to continue that counts... Winston Churchill

_____

_____

_____

_____

_____

_____

_____

_____

_____

_____

_____

_____

_____

_____

_____

_____

_____

_____

_____

_____

53.   Try not to become a man of success, but rather try to become a man of value... Albert Einstein

_____

_____

_____

_____

_____

_____

_____

_____

_____

_____

_____

_____

_____

_____

_____

_____

_____

_____

_____

_____

54. If everyone is moving forward together, then success takes care of itself... Henry Ford

55.   Success is a science; if you have the conditions, you get the result... Oscar Wilde

_____

_____

_____

_____

_____

_____

_____

_____

_____

_____

_____

_____

_____

_____

_____

_____

_____

_____

_____

_____

_____

56.   Success depends upon previous preparation, and without such preparation there is sure to be failure... Confucius

_____

_____

_____

_____

_____

_____

_____

_____

_____

_____

_____

_____

_____

_____

_____

_____

_____

_____

57.   Discipline is the soul of an army. It makes small numbers formidable; procures success to the weak, and esteem to all... George Washington

_____

_____

_____

_____

_____

_____

_____

_____

_____

_____

_____

_____

_____

_____

_____

_____

_____

_____

_____

58.	There is no way to happiness. Happiness is the way...
Thich Nhat Hanh

_____

_____

_____

_____

_____

_____

_____

_____

_____

_____

_____

_____

_____

_____

_____

_____

_____

_____

_____

_____

59.   If you wish to be a success in the world, promise everything, deliver nothing... Napoleon Bonaparte

_____

_____

_____

_____

_____

_____

_____

_____

_____

_____

_____

_____

_____

_____

_____

_____

_____

_____

60.   The most important single ingredient in the formula of success is knowing how to get along with people... Theodore Roosevelt

_____

_____

_____

_____

_____

_____

_____

_____

_____

_____

_____

_____

_____

_____

_____

_____

_____

_____

61.   Success in management requires learning as fast as the world is changing... Warren Bennis

62.   The power of imagination makes us infinite... John Muir

63.   Money won't create success, the freedom to make it will... Nelson Mandela

_____

_____

_____

_____

_____

_____

_____

_____

_____

_____

_____

_____

_____

_____

_____

_____

_____

_____

_____

64.   All Birds find shelter during a rain. But Eagle avoids rain by flying above the Clouds... APJ Abdul Kalam

_____

_____

_____

_____

_____

_____

_____

_____

_____

_____

_____

_____

_____

_____

_____

_____

_____

_____

_____

65.   The key to success is action, and the essential in action is perseverance... Sun Yat-sen

_____

_____

_____

_____

_____

_____

_____

_____

_____

_____

_____

_____

_____

_____

_____

_____

_____

_____

_____

66. Success is simply a matter of luck. Ask any failure... Earl Wilson

_____

_____

_____

_____

_____

_____

_____

_____

_____

_____

_____

_____

_____

_____

_____

_____

_____

_____

67.   Success is dependent on effort... Sophocles

_____

_____

_____

_____

_____

_____

_____

_____

_____

_____

_____

_____

_____

_____

_____

_____

_____

_____

_____

_____

_____

68.   Things work out best for those who make the best of how things work out... John Wooden

_____

_____

_____

_____

_____

_____

_____

_____

_____

_____

_____

_____

_____

_____

_____

_____

_____

_____

_____

_____

69.   I destroy my enemies when I make them my friends...
Abraham Lincoln

70.   All our dreams can come true if we have the courage to pursue them... Walt Disney

_____

_____

_____

_____

_____

_____

_____

_____

_____

_____

_____

_____

_____

_____

_____

_____

_____

_____

71.   Whenever you find yourself on the side of the majority, it is time to pause and reflect... Mark Twain

_____

_____

_____

_____

_____

_____

_____

_____

_____

_____

_____

_____

_____

_____

_____

_____

_____

_____

72.   You may have to fight a battle more than once to win it... Margaret Thatcher

73. Creativity is intelligence having fun... Albert Einstein

74.   What you get by achieving your goals is not as important as what you become by achieving your goals...
Henry David Thoreau

75.   A comfort zone is a beautiful place, but nothing ever grows there... Unknown

_____

_____

_____

_____

_____

_____

_____

_____

_____

_____

_____

_____

_____

_____

_____

_____

_____

_____

_____

76.   Do it with passion, or not at all... Rosa Nouchette Carey

_____

_____

_____

_____

_____

_____

_____

_____

_____

_____

_____

_____

_____

_____

_____

_____

_____

_____

_____

77.   Most of the important things in the world have been accomplished by people who have kept on trying when there seemed to be no help at all... Dale Carnegie

_____

_____

_____

_____

_____

_____

_____

_____

_____

_____

_____

_____

_____

_____

_____

_____

_____

_____

_____

78.　　The journey of a thousand miles begins with one step...
Lao Tzu

_____

_____

_____

_____

_____

_____

_____

_____

_____

_____

_____

_____

_____

_____

_____

_____

_____

_____

_____

79.   What you do speaks so loudly that I cannot hear what you say... Ralph Waldo Emerson

_____

_____

_____

_____

_____

_____

_____

_____

_____

_____

_____

_____

_____

_____

_____

_____

_____

_____

_____

_____

80.   Keep your face to the sunshine and you can never see the shadow... Helen Keller

_____

_____

_____

_____

_____

_____

_____

_____

_____

_____

_____

_____

_____

_____

_____

_____

_____

_____

81.   The best way out is always through... Robert Frost

_____

_____

_____

_____

_____

_____

_____

_____

_____

_____

_____

_____

_____

_____

_____

_____

_____

_____

_____

82.   Every moment is a fresh beginning... T.S. Eliot

_____
_____
_____
_____
_____
_____
_____
_____
_____
_____
_____
_____
_____
_____
_____
_____
_____
_____
_____
_____

83.   Everything you've ever wanted is on the other side of fear... George Addair

_____

_____

_____

_____

_____

_____

_____

_____

_____

_____

_____

_____

_____

_____

_____

_____

_____

_____

_____

_____

_____

_____

_____

84.   I love to see a young girl go out and grab the world by the lapels. Life's a bitch. You've got to go out and kick ass...
Maya Angelou

85.   No masterpiece was ever created by a lazy artist...
Anonymous

86.   Innovation distinguishes between a leader and a follower... Steve Jobs

_____

_____

_____

_____

_____

_____

_____

_____

_____

_____

_____

_____

_____

_____

_____

_____

_____

_____

_____

87.   I find that the harder I work, the more luck I seem to have... Thomas Jefferson

_____

_____

_____

_____

_____

_____

_____

_____

_____

_____

_____

_____

_____

_____

_____

_____

_____

88.   If you don't design your own life plan, chances are you'll fall into someone else's plan. And guess what they have planned for you? Not much... Jim Rohn

_____

_____

_____

_____

_____

_____

_____

_____

_____

_____

_____

_____

_____

_____

_____

_____

_____

_____

_____

89.   The most effective way to do it, is to do it... Amelia
Earhart

_____

_____

_____

_____

_____

_____

_____

_____

_____

_____

_____

_____

_____

_____

_____

_____

_____

_____

_____

90.   Defeat is not the worst of failures. Not to have tried is the true failure... George Edward Woodberry

_____

_____

_____

_____

_____

_____

_____

_____

_____

_____

_____

_____

_____

_____

_____

_____

_____

_____

_____

91.   To accomplish great things, we must not only act, but also dream, not only plan, but also believe... Anatole France

_____

_____

_____

_____

_____

_____

_____

_____

_____

_____

_____

_____

_____

_____

_____

_____

_____

_____

_____

92.   Success seems to be connected with action. Successful people keep moving. They make mistakes, but they don't quit... Conrad Hilton

_____

_____

_____

_____

_____

_____

_____

_____

_____

_____

_____

_____

_____

_____

_____

_____

93.   The tragedy in life doesn't lie in not reaching your goal. The tragedy lies in having no goal to reach... Benjamin Mays

94.   The secret of joy in work is contained in one word: excellence. To know how to do something well is to enjoy it...
Pearl Buck

_____

_____

_____

_____

_____

_____

_____

_____

_____

_____

_____

_____

_____

_____

_____

_____

_____

_____

_____

95. Knowing trees, I understand the meaning of patience. Knowing grass, I can appreciate persistence... Hal Borland

96.   Be patient with yourself. Self growth is tender; it's holy ground. There's no greater investment... Stephen Covey

97.   One who asks is a fool for five minutes, but one who does not ask remains a fool forever... Chinese Proverb

_____

_____

_____

_____

_____

_____

_____

_____

_____

_____

_____

_____

_____

_____

_____

_____

_____

_____

98.   Yesterday is not ours to recover, but tomorrow is ours to win or lose... Lyndon Johnson

_____
_____
_____
_____
_____
_____
_____
_____
_____
_____
_____
_____
_____
_____
_____
_____
_____
_____
_____
_____

99.   Formal education will make you a living; self-education will make you a fortune... Jim Rohn

100.   Nothing is impossible; the word itself says I'm possible... Audrey Hepburn

_____

_____

_____

_____

_____

_____

_____

_____

_____

_____

_____

_____

_____

_____

_____

_____

_____